Recycling

LEVEL 9

Teaching Tips

Gold Level 9

This book focuses on developing reading independence, fluency, and comprehension.

Before Reading

- Ask readers what they think the book will be about based on the title. Have them support their answer.

Read the Book

- Encourage readers to read silently on their own.
- As readers encounter unfamiliar words, ask them to look for context clues to see if they can figure out what the words mean. Encourage them to locate boldfaced words in the glossary and ask questions to clarify the meaning of new vocabulary.
- Allow readers time to absorb the text and think about each chapter.
- Ask readers to write down any questions they have about the book's content.

After Reading

- Ask readers to summarize the book.
- Encourage them to point out anything they did not understand and ask questions.
- Ask readers to review the questions on page 23. Have them go back through the book to find answers. Have them write their answers on a separate sheet of paper.

© 2024 Booklife Publishing
This edition is published by arrangement with Booklife Publishing.

North American adaptations © 2024 Jump!
5357 Penn Avenue South
Minneapolis, MN 55419
www.jumplibrary.com

Decodables by Jump! are published by Jump! Library.
All rights reserved. No part of this book may be reproduced in any form without written permission from the publisher.

Library of Congress Cataloging-in-Publication Data is available at www.loc.gov or upon request from the publisher.

ISBN: 979-8-88524-796-2 (hardcover)
ISBN: 979-8-88524-797-9 (paperback)
ISBN: 979-8-88524-798-6 (ebook)

Photo Credits

Images are courtesy of Shutterstock.com. With thanks to Getty Images, Thinkstock Photo and iStockphoto. Cover – Inside Creative House. p4–5 – Halfpoint, MPIX. p6–7 – SERGEI BRIK, Mandic Photos. p8–9 – Rawpixel.com, wanwan14. p10–11 – Laszlo66, Inna Reznik. p12–13 – Quang Ho, LI CHAOSHU. p14–15 – teatian, gabriel12. p16–17 – rodimov, KKulikov. p18–19 – zzcapture, MOHAMED ABDULRAHEEM. p20–21 – wavebreakmedia, Extarz.

Table of Contents

Recycling Journeys

When we throw something away, it goes into a **landfill**. Landfill sites are huge pits where we dump everybody's trash. Landfills are not good for our planet.

Instead of throwing something we don't need into landfill sites, we can usually **recycle** it. This means turning it into something brand new. Let's look at the recycling journeys of some objects.

The Journey of an Aluminum Can

Lots of people love a can of soda. But **aluminum** cans are made to be used once, then thrown away. This is known as a **single-use item**.

You can't reseal a can and use it for drinking again. So, what can you do with all these cans? You can put them into a recycling bin! This means they will be sent off to be made into something new.

The metal that cans are made from is aluminum. Aluminum can be recycled again and again, forever! Rinse cans with water to make sure they are clean and not sticky. Then, put them in a recycling bin.

Aluminum cans go to the **recycling center**. Then, the cans are washed and cut into small pieces. The small pieces are melted down into new metal. The new metal is shaped and made into new cans.

The Journey of a Piece of Paper

Paper is made from trees. Trees are cut down and turned into a sticky, wet **pulp**. The pulp is dried out in thin sheets and turned into paper. We use paper for lots of things.

Paper is great for drawing or painting on. However, when you have drawn on your paper or drunk from your paper cup, its job is finished. Many paper items cannot be used more than once. This means paper items are often single-use items.

When we put paper into a landfill, it starts to break down over time. However, when it breaks down, it releases something called **methane**. This can be bad for the planet. No need to panic, though. We can recycle paper too!

At recycling centers, old paper is washed and made into a watery paste called pulp. The pulp is mixed with new paper, then turned into large, thin sheets. Once dry, it is rolled up to be made into new things.

The Journey of a Glass Jar

Glass jars are useful containers. Maybe you've seen them in stores, full of jam or sauce? When they are empty, glass jars can be washed and used again. If you are finished with them, they can be recycled.

Other materials break down more quickly, but glass does not. If we throw glass into a landfill, it will stay there for a very long time. However, they don't need to go to a landfill. They can be put into a recycling bin.

When you are finished with your glass jar, you must wash it to remove any food, glue, or paint. You should also take off the lid and remove the label. Once collected, it will be taken to a recycling center.

Glass is sorted by type and color. Then, it is smashed into small pieces. The smashed glass is melted, and new glass is made. This new glass is formed into new bottles, jars, and other items, ready to be used again.

The Journey of a Plastic Bottle

Plastic bottles are something we use all the time. They are not heavy, so they are easy to carry around. Unlike a glass jar, plastic bottles are not made to be used again. They are another single-use item.

Plastic bottles are easy to throw away. One way that plastic bottles are like glass jars is that they take a very long time to break down. This means we should avoid putting them into a landfill.

Luckily, plastic bottles can be recycled. Once your plastic bottle is empty, you should wash it out to make sure it's clean. They can be collected and turned into new plastic but only a few times.

When you send it for recycling, it is sorted by color and then washed. The plastic is then either cut or melted into small pieces. These small pieces are turned into pellets of new plastic. These are heated up and shaped into new objects.

Index

How to Use an Index

An index helps us find information in a book. Each word has a set of page numbers. These page numbers are where you can find information about that word.

Page numbers

Example: balloons 5, 8–10, 19

Important word

This means page 8, page 10, and all the pages in between. Here, it means pages 8, 9, and 10.

Questions

1. What is a single-use item?

2. How many times can aluminum be recycled?

3. How is glass sorted?

4. Can you use the Table of Contents to find which pages have information about how paper is made?

5. Can you use the Index to find information about methane in the book?

6. Using the Glossary, can you define what a landfill is?

Glossary

aluminum:
A light, silver-colored metal.

landfill:
A large area where trash is buried.

methane:
A colorless and odorless gas.

pulp:
Any soft, wet mixture.

recycle:
To process old items such as glass, paper, and aluminum so they can be used to make new products.

recycling center:
Facilities where recycled items are sent and sorted.

single-use item:
Something that is only used once before it is recycled or thrown away.